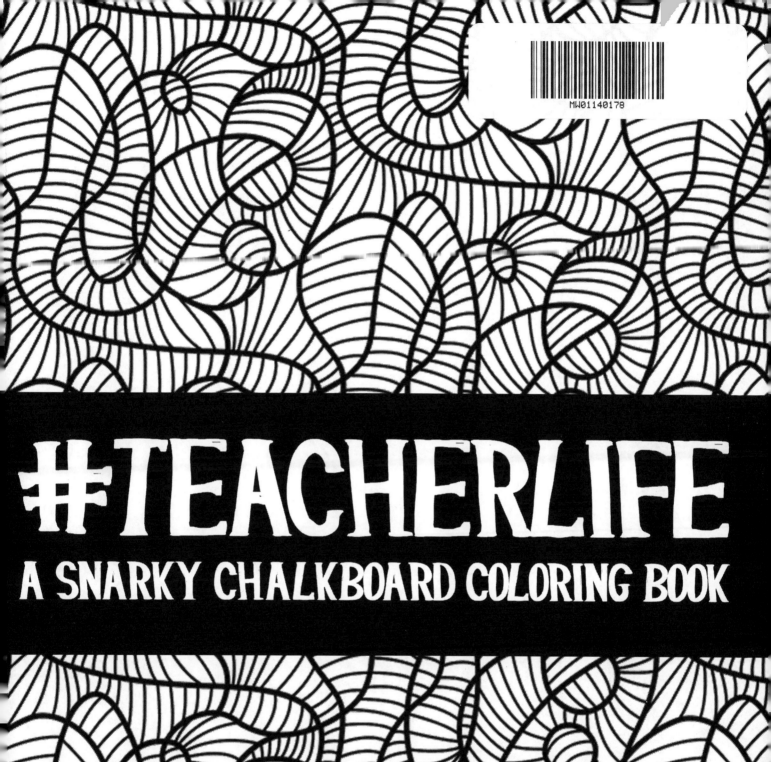

# #TEACHERLIFE
## A SNARKY CHALKBOARD COLORING BOOK

# Illustrated by Micaela

ISBN-13: 978-1533134066
ISBN-10: 1533134065

# FREE DOWNLOAD

www.papeteriebleu.com/teacherlife

**YOUR DOWNLOAD CODE: TCH6545**

 @papeteriebleu

 Papeterie Bleu

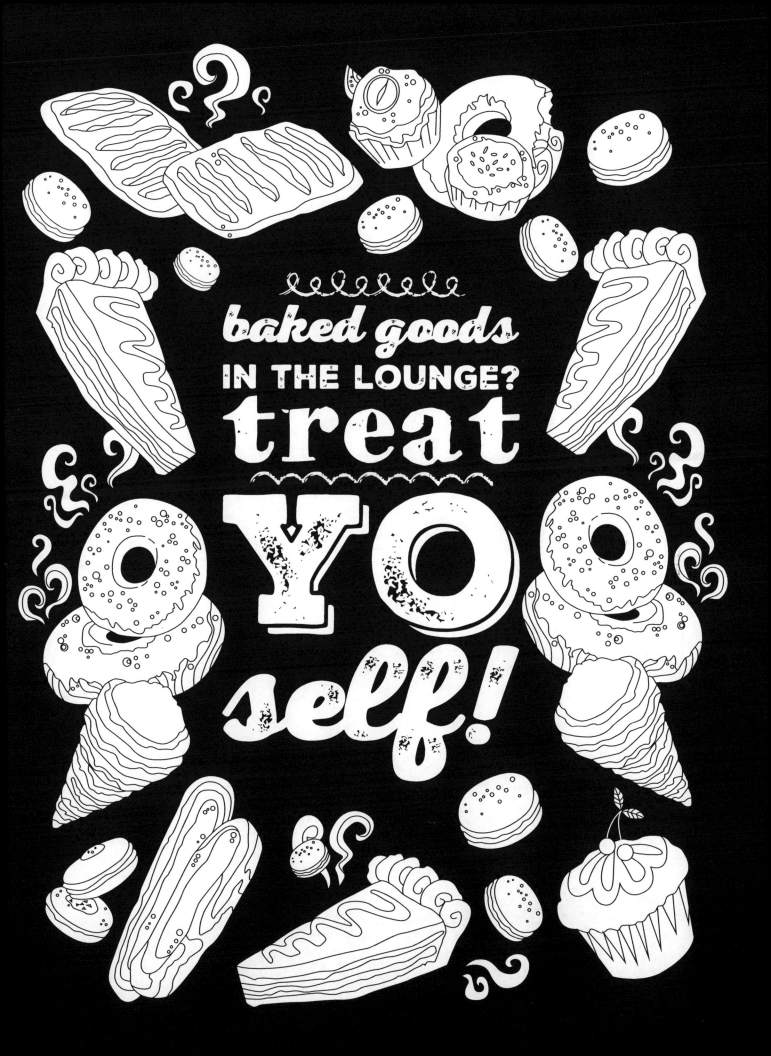

$$E = mc^2$$

$$\oint \vec{D}\,d\vec{S} = Q$$

$$E = \hbar k^2$$

$$Q = mC\Delta t$$

$$\oint \vec{B}\,d\vec{\ell} = \mu_0 \sum I_i$$

$$PV = nRT$$

$$E_k = \frac{1}{2}mv^2$$

$$E = \hbar\omega$$

$$\omega = 2\pi f$$

$$M = Fd\cos\alpha$$

$$\lambda \cdot T = b$$

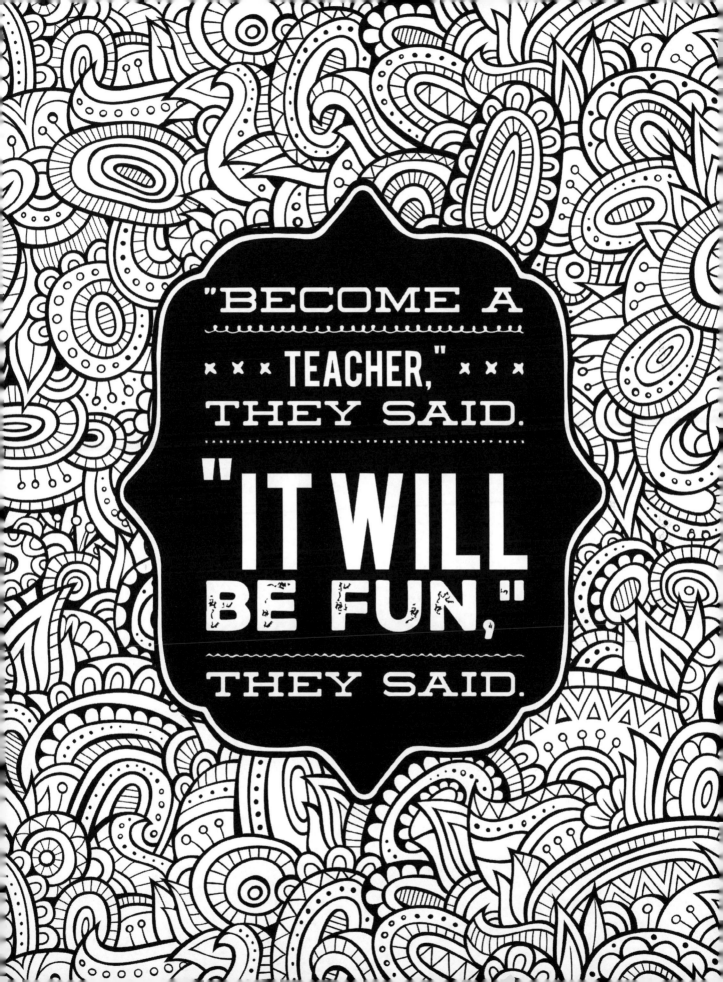

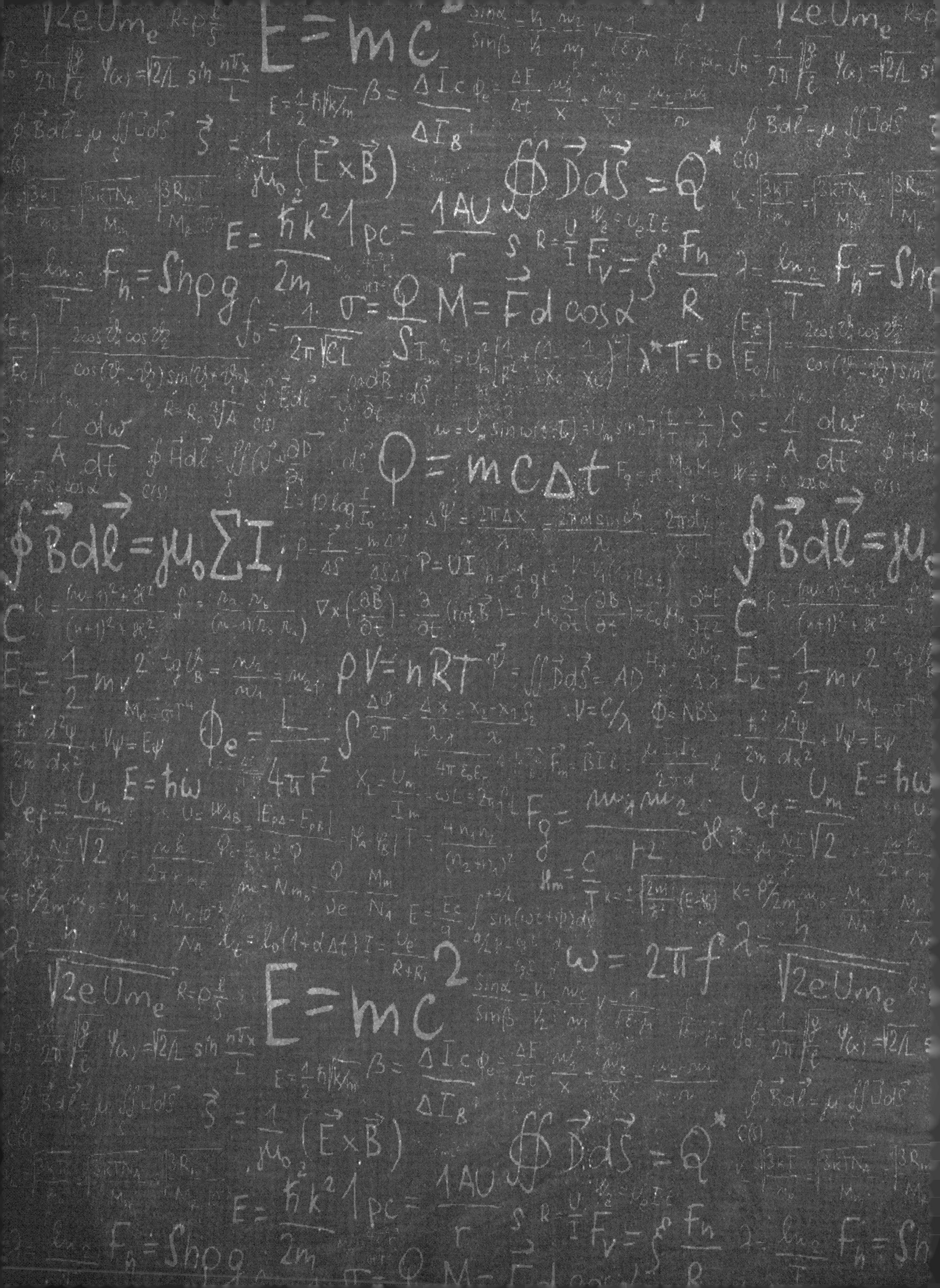
E=mc²
Q=mcΔt
pV=nRT
ω=2πf
E=ħω
M=Fd cosα
λ*T=b
P=UI
Φ=NBS

$$E = mc^2$$

$$\oint \vec{D}\,d\vec{S} = Q^*$$

$$E = \hbar k^2 \quad 1pc = \frac{1AU}{r}$$

$$F_n = Shpg \quad \frac{1}{2m}$$

$$M = Fd\cos\alpha \quad \lambda^* T = b$$

$$Q = mc\Delta t$$

$$\oint \vec{B}\,d\vec{l} = \mu_0 \sum I_i$$

$$PV = nRT$$

$$E_k = \frac{1}{2}mv^2$$

$$E = \hbar\omega$$

$$\omega = 2\pi f$$

$$E = mc^2$$

HAPPINESS IS

A THREE

DAY

WEEKEND

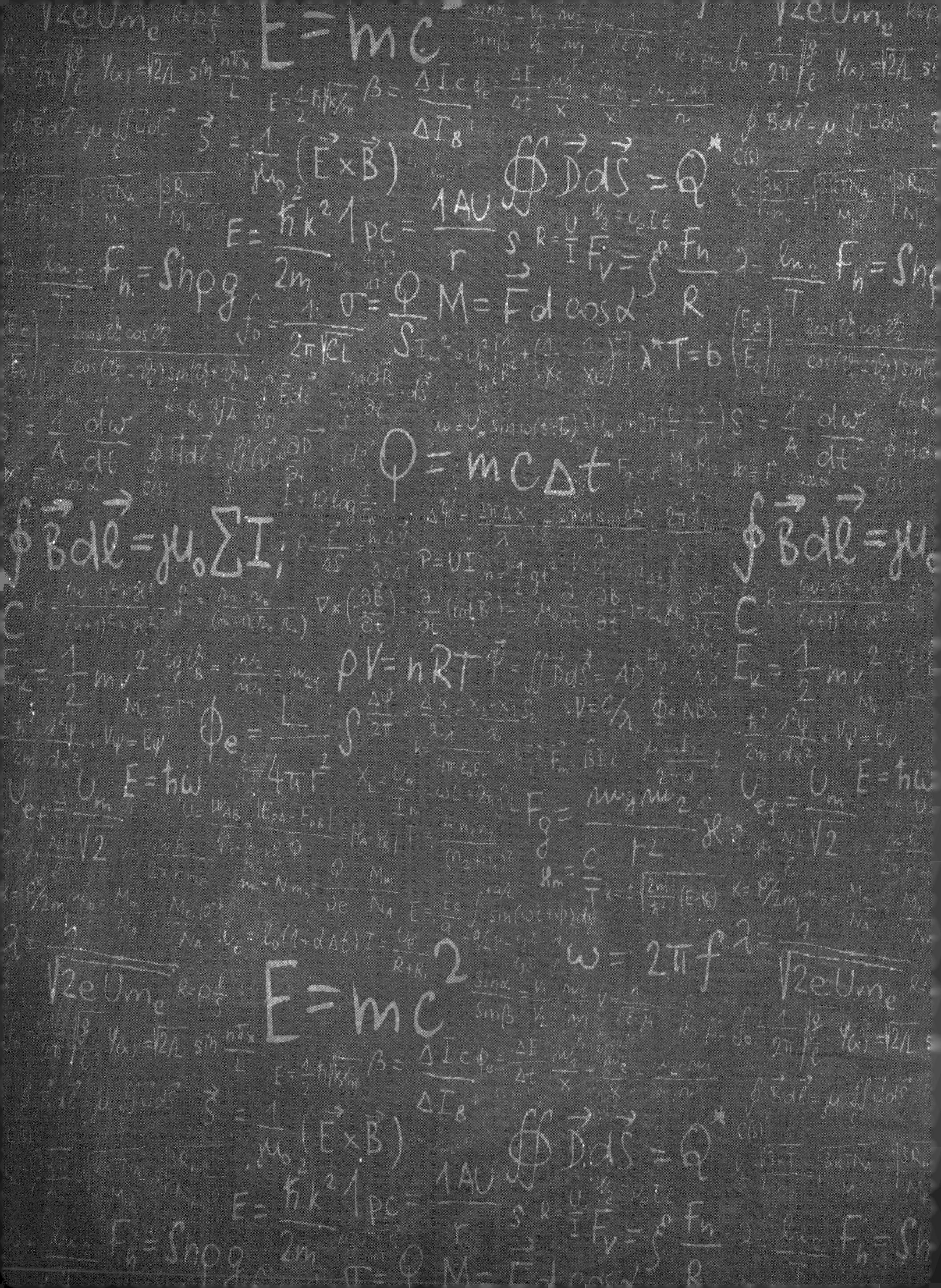
E=mc²
Q=mcΔt
ρV=nRT
E=ħω
ω=2πf

Every day I wonder:
WILL TODAY
BE THE DAY
I ACCIDENTALLY
SCREAM OUT LOUD,
instead of
IN MY HEAD.

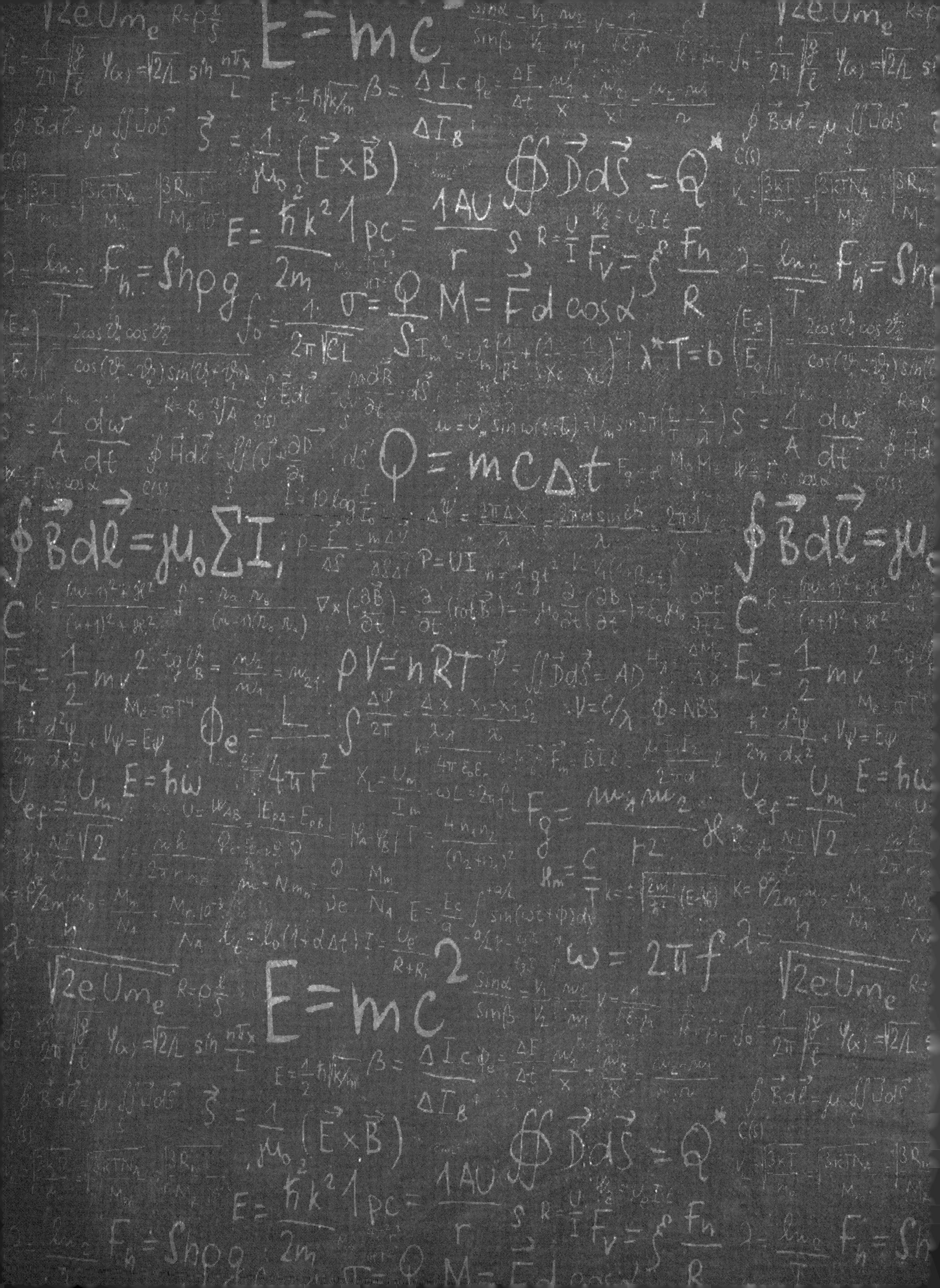

E=mc
Q=mcΔt
pV=nRT
ω=2πf
E=mc²

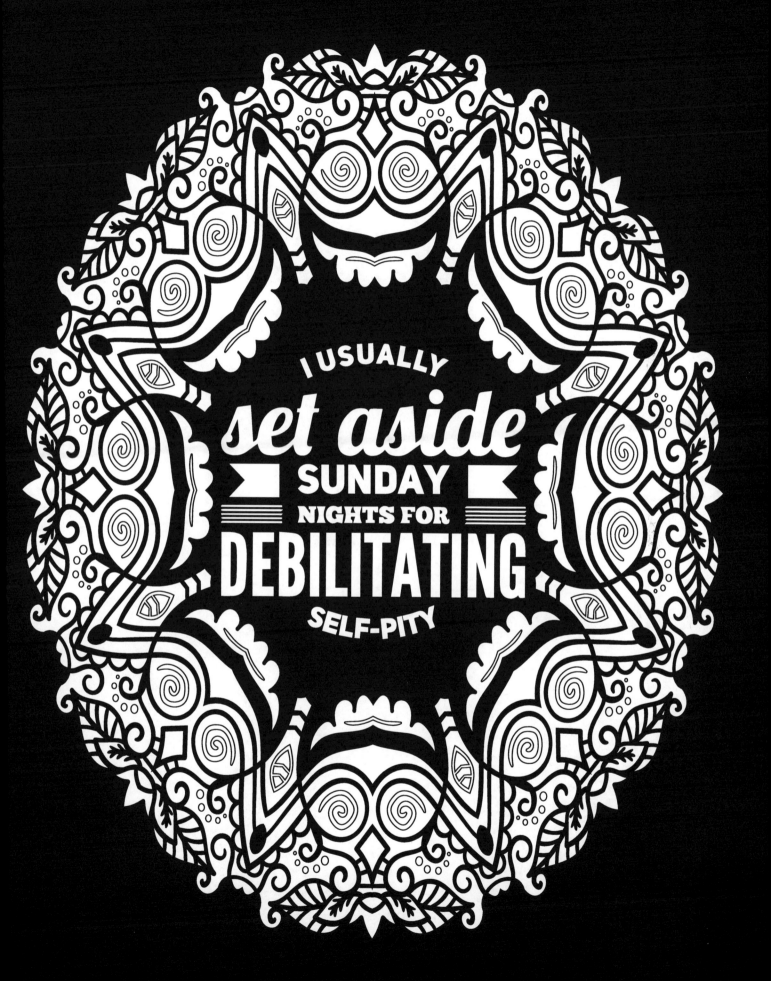

$$E = mc^2$$

$$\oint \vec{D}\,d\vec{S} = Q$$

$$E = \hbar k^2 \qquad 1\,pc = \frac{1AU}{r}$$

$$Q = mc\Delta t$$

$$\oint \vec{B}\,d\vec{l} = \mu_0 \sum I_i$$

$$PV = nRT$$

$$E = \frac{1}{2}mv^2$$

$$E = \hbar\omega$$

$$\omega = 2\pi f$$

$$E = mc^2$$

$$\lambda \cdot T = b$$

$$M = Fd\cos\alpha$$

$$\oint \vec{D}\,d\vec{S} = Q$$

$$\Phi = NBS$$

$$E = mc^2$$

$$\oint \vec{D}\,d\vec{S} = Q$$

$$E = \hbar k^2 \qquad 1PC = \frac{1AU}{r}$$

$$\frac{2m}{} \qquad f_0 = \frac{1}{2\pi\sqrt{CL}} \qquad \sigma = \frac{\Phi}{S} \qquad M = Fd\cos\alpha$$

$$Q = mc\Delta t$$

$$\oint \vec{B}\,d\vec{l} = \mu_0 \sum I \qquad P = UI$$

$$\oint \vec{B}\,d\vec{l} = \mu_0$$

$$PV = nRT \qquad \iint \vec{D}\,d\vec{S} = AD \qquad E_k = \frac{1}{2}mv^2$$

$$\Phi_e \qquad \upsilon = C/\lambda \qquad \Phi_0 = NBS$$

$$E = \hbar\omega \qquad E = \hbar\omega$$

$$E = mc^2 \qquad \omega = 2\pi f$$

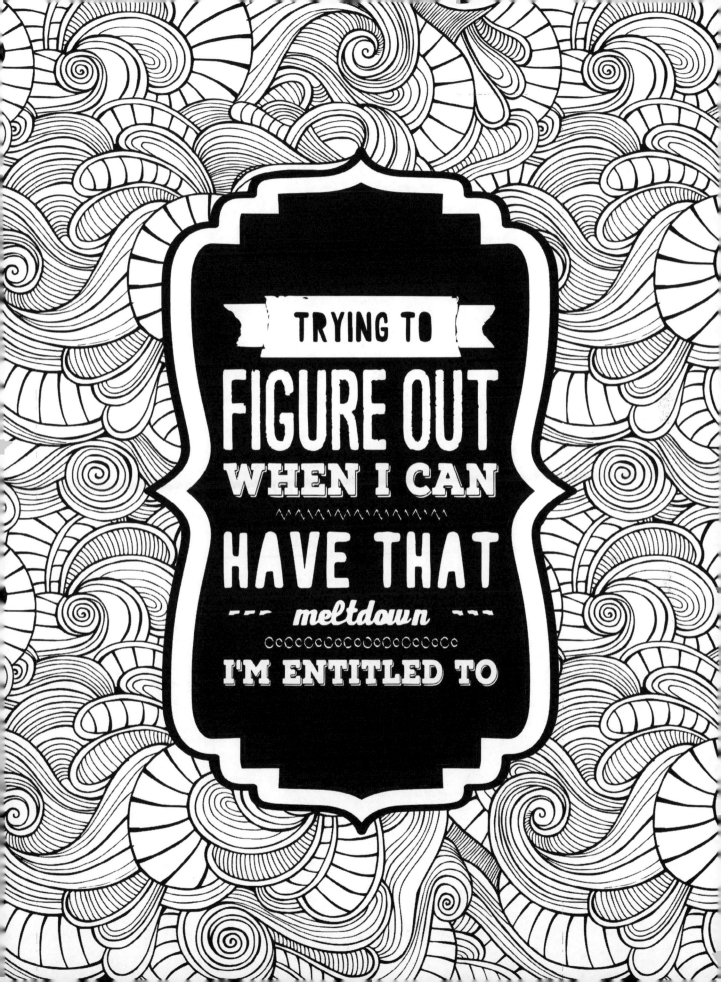

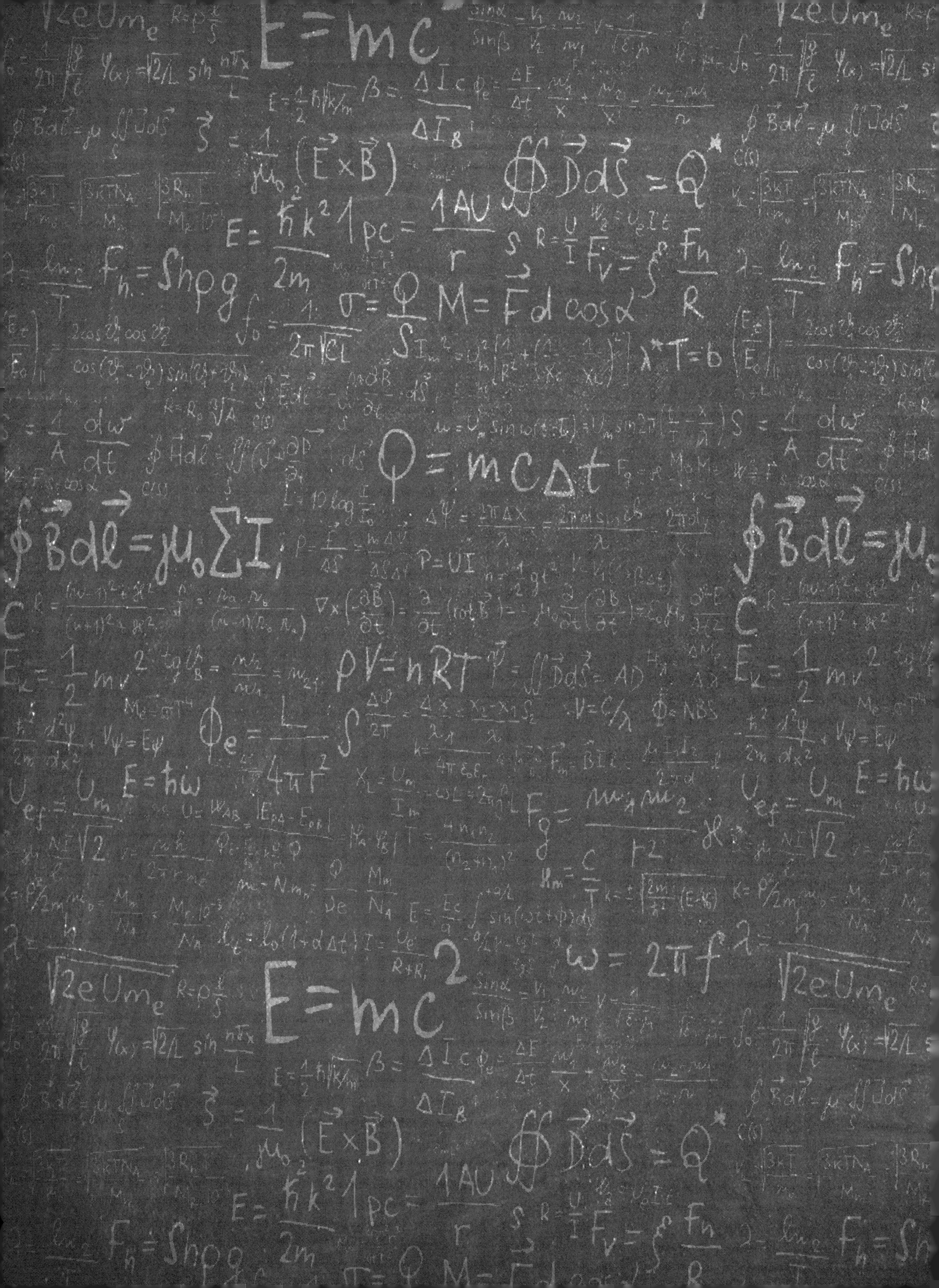
E=mc²
Q=mcΔt
pV=nRT
ω=2πf
E=ħω

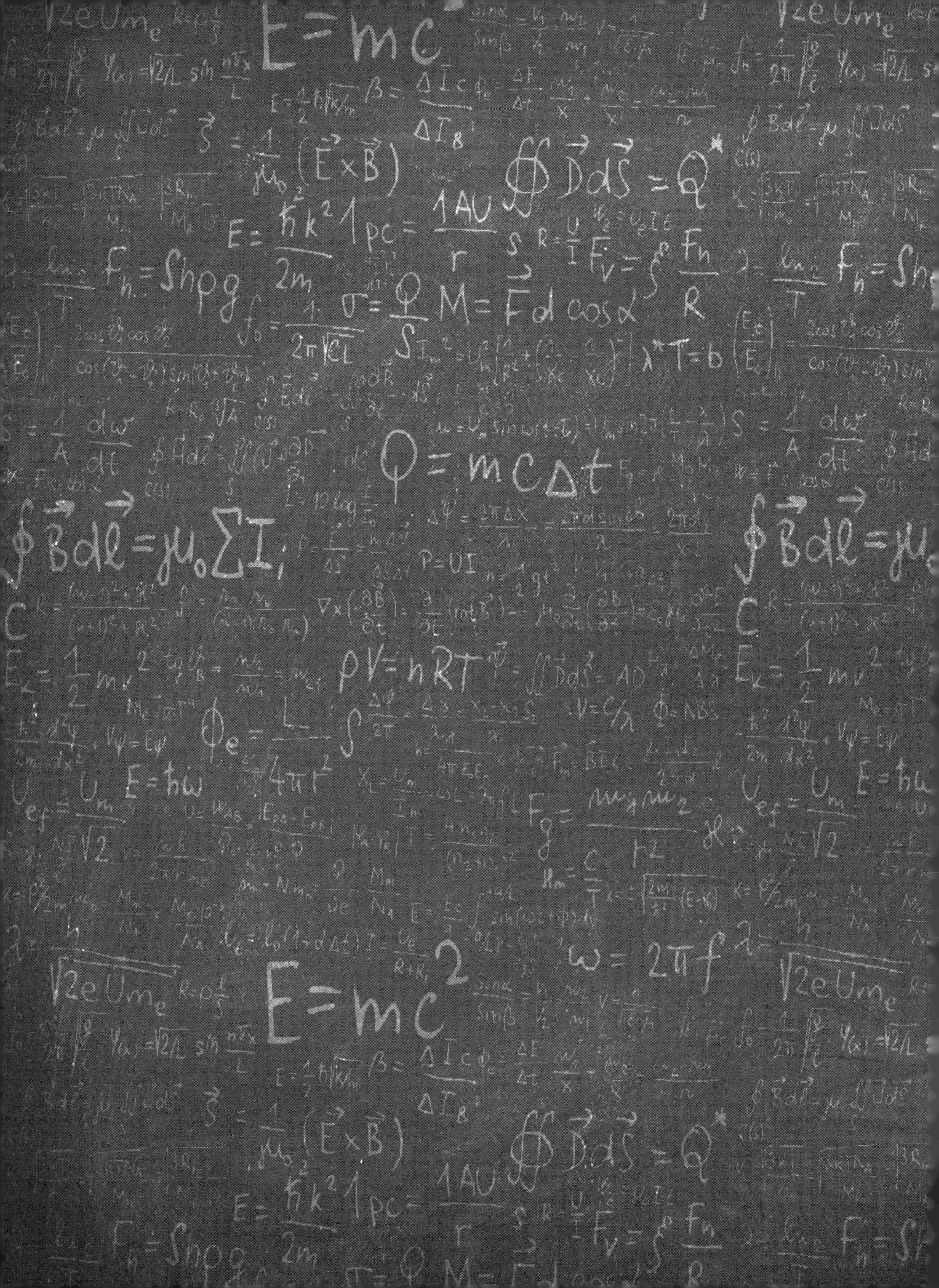
E=mc2
Q=mcΔt
pV=nRT
ω=2πf
M=Fd cos α
λ*T=b
P=UI
Φ=NBS
E=ħω

$$E = mc^2$$

$$\vec{S} = \frac{1}{\mu_0}(\vec{E} \times \vec{B})$$

$$\oint \vec{D}\,d\vec{S} = Q^*$$

$$E = \frac{\hbar^2 k^2}{2m} \quad 1\,pc = \frac{1\,AU}{r}$$

$$F_n = Sh\rho g \qquad \sigma = \frac{Q}{S} \quad M = Fd\cos\alpha \qquad \lambda^* T = b$$

$$f_0 = \frac{1}{2\pi\sqrt{CL}}$$

$$Q = mc\Delta t$$

$$\oint \vec{B}\,d\vec{\ell} = \mu_0 \sum I$$

$$PV = nRT \qquad \iint \vec{D}\,d\vec{S} = AD$$

$$E_k = \frac{1}{2}mv^2$$

$$\phi_e = \int E$$

$$E = \hbar\omega$$

$$\omega = 2\pi f$$

$$E = mc^2$$

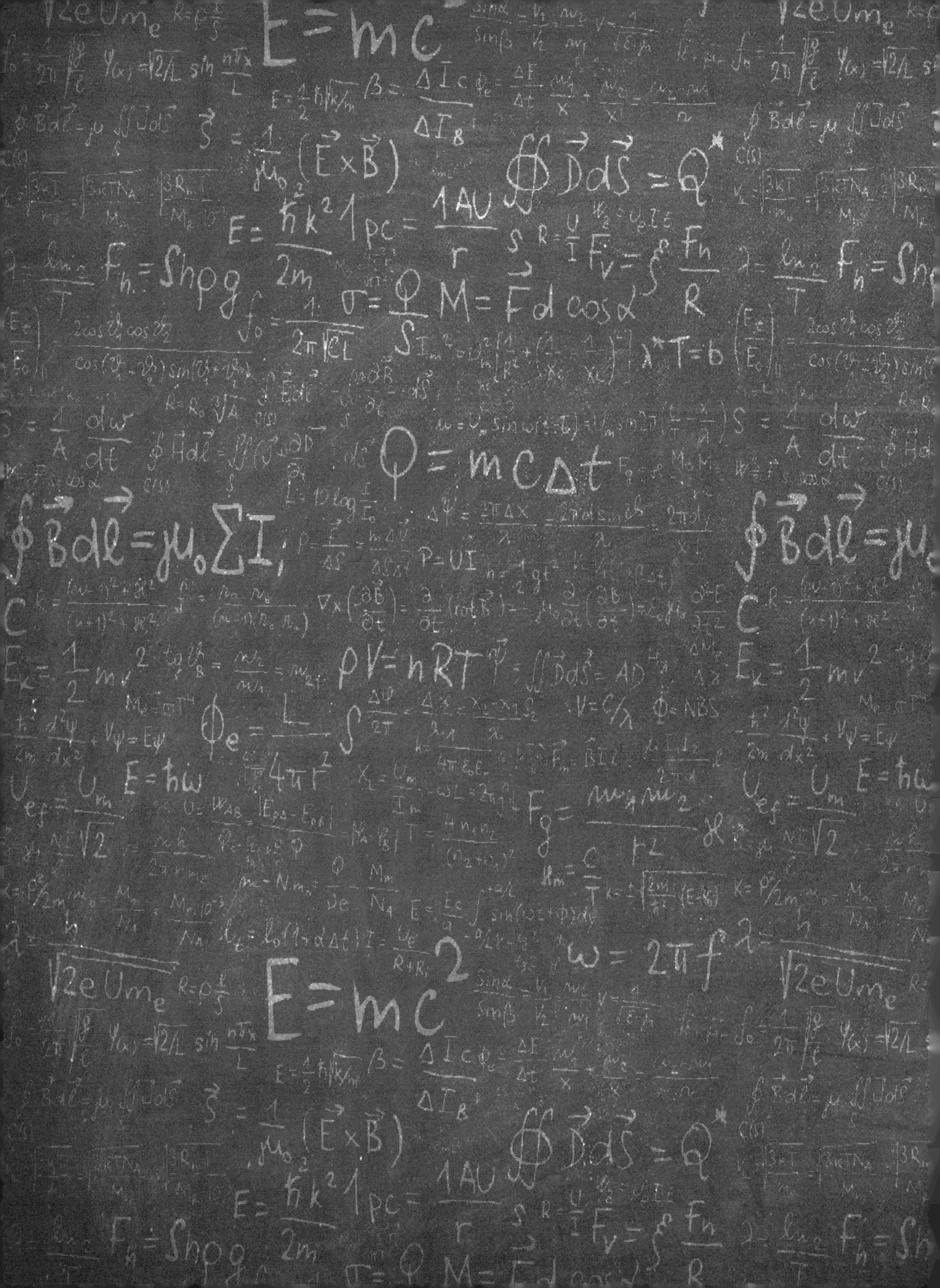

E=mc²
Q=mcΔt
ρV=nRT
ω=2πf
E=ħω

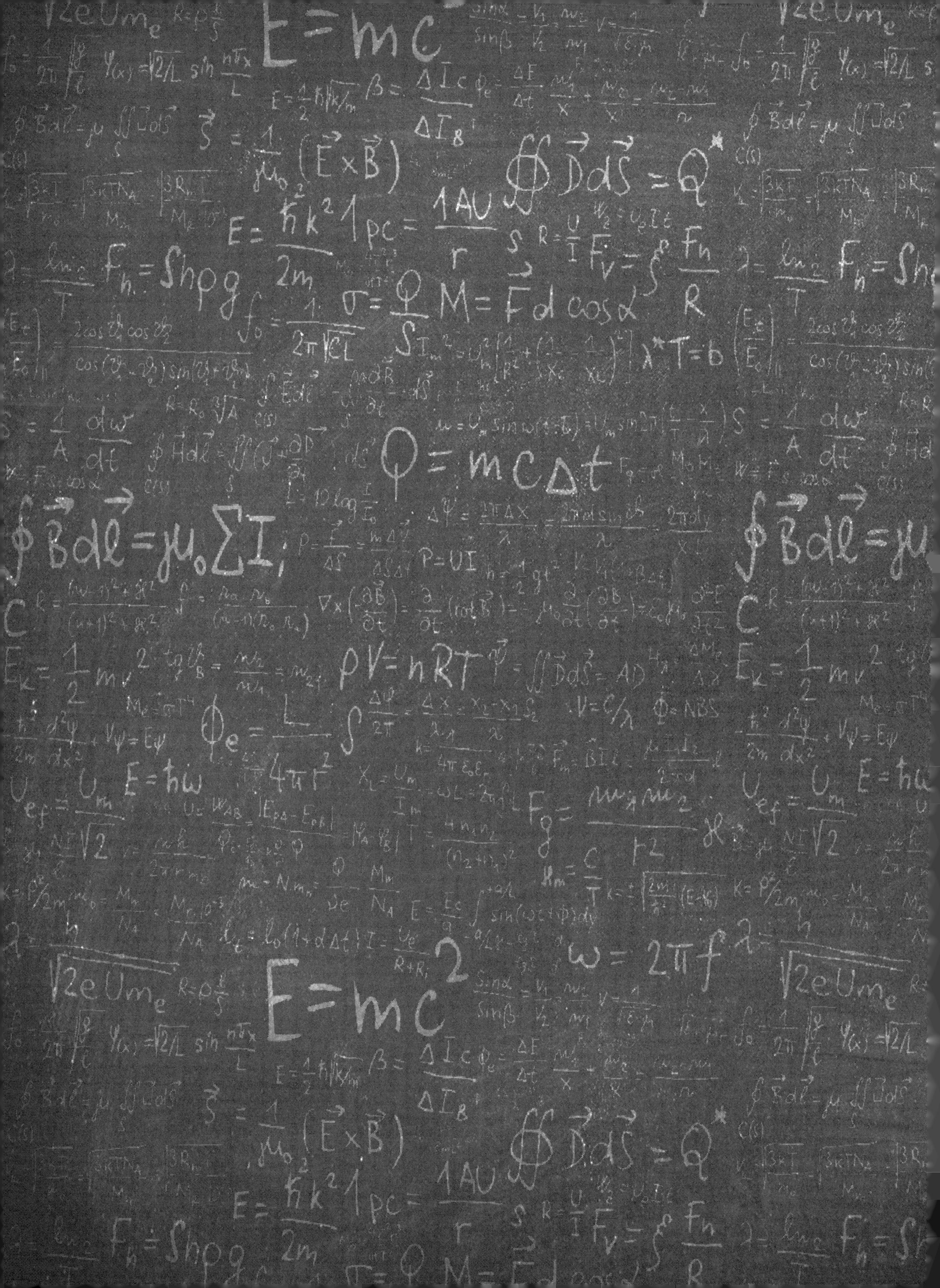
E=mc2
Q=mcΔt
pV=nRT
ω=2πf
E=mc2

$$E = mc^2$$

$$\Psi(x) = \sqrt{2/L}\ \sin\frac{n\pi x}{L}$$

$$\vec{S} = \frac{1}{\mu_0}(\vec{E}\times\vec{B})$$

$$\oiint \vec{D}\,d\vec{S} = Q^*$$

$$E = \hbar k^2 \qquad 1\,pc = \frac{1AU}{r}$$

$$f_n = Sh\rho g \qquad \frac{1}{2m}$$

$$\sigma = \frac{Q}{S} \qquad M = Fd\cos\alpha$$

$$f_0 = \frac{1}{2\pi\sqrt{CL}}$$

$$\lambda^* T = b$$

$$Q = mc\Delta t$$

$$\oint \vec{B}\,d\vec{l} = \mu_0 \sum I_i$$

$$\oint \vec{B}\,d\vec{l} = \mu$$

$$PV = nRT$$

$$\iint \vec{D}\,d\vec{S} = \Delta D$$

$$E_2 = \frac{1}{2}mv^2$$

$$E = \frac{1}{2}mv^2$$

$$\Phi e = L = \int$$

$$E = \hbar\omega$$

$$4\pi r^2$$

$$\Phi_e = NBS$$

$$\omega = 2\pi f$$

$$E = mc^2$$

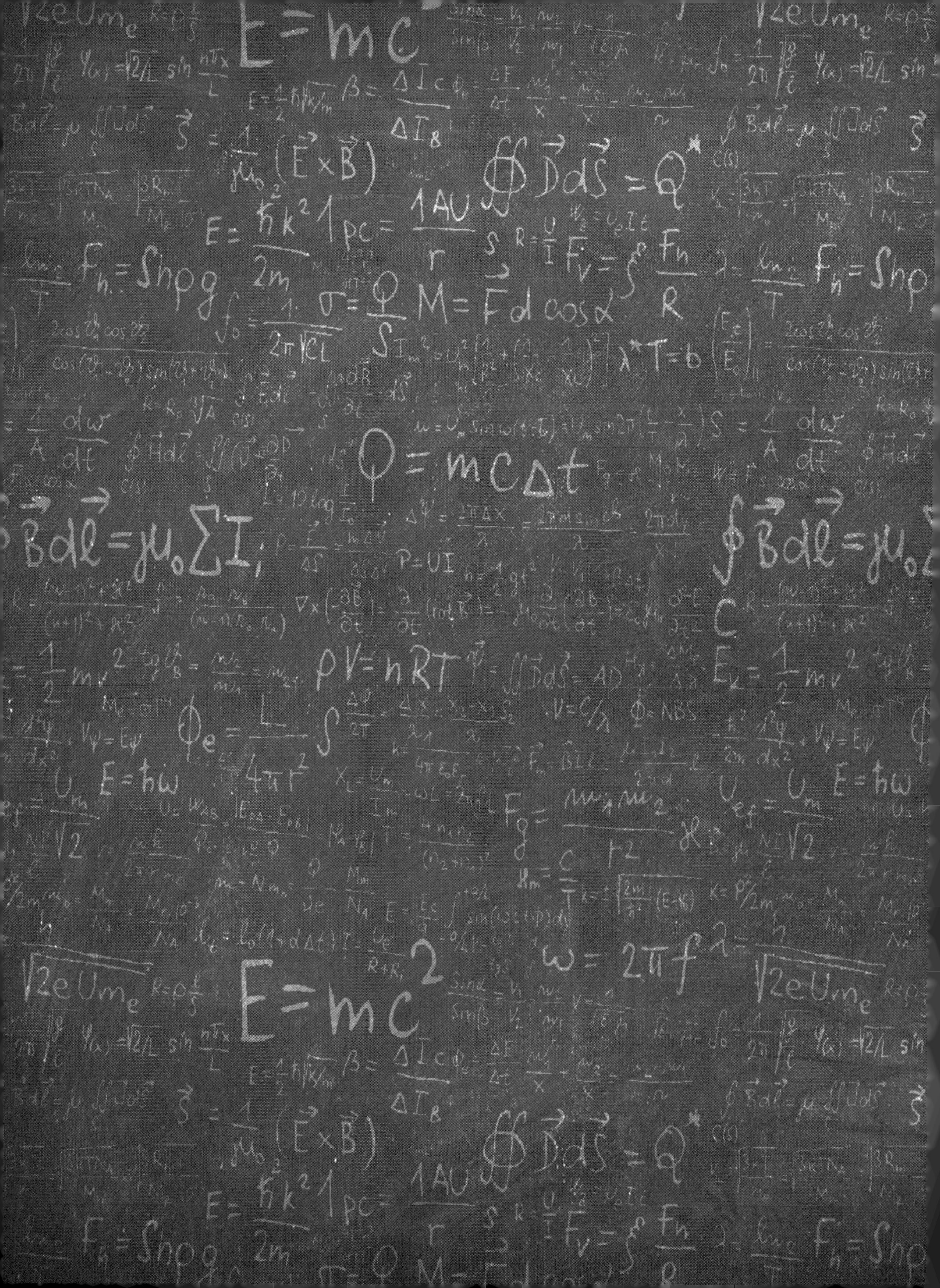
E=mc2
Q=mcΔt
pV=nRT
ω=2πf
E=ħω
M=Fd cosα

$$E = mc^2$$

$$\psi(x) = \sqrt{2/L}\,\sin\frac{n\pi x}{L}$$

$$\vec{S} = \frac{1}{\mu_0}(\vec{E}\times\vec{B})$$

$$\oiint \vec{D}\,d\vec{S} = Q^*$$

$$E = \frac{\hbar k^2}{2m} \qquad 1\,pc = \frac{1\,AU}{r}$$

$$f_n = \mathcal{S}n\rho g$$

$$M = Fd\cos\alpha$$

$$\lambda^* T = b$$

$$Q = mc\Delta t$$

$$\oint \vec{B}\,d\vec{\ell} = \mu_0 \sum I$$

$$PV = nRT$$

$$E_k = \frac{1}{2}mv^2$$

$$E = \hbar\omega$$

$$\omega = 2\pi f$$

$$\sqrt{2eU m_e}$$

$$E = mc^2$$

$$\oiint \vec{D}\,d\vec{S} = Q$$

$$E = \frac{\hbar k^2}{2m}$$

$$1\,pc = \frac{1\,AU}{r}$$

$$M = Fd\cos\alpha$$

$$\lambda \cdot T = b$$

$$Q = mc\Delta t$$

$$\oint \vec{B}\,d\vec{\ell} = \mu_0 \sum I$$

$$P = UI$$

$$PV = nRT$$

$$\Phi = NBS$$

$$E_k = \frac{1}{2}mv^2$$

$$E = \hbar\omega$$

$$\omega = 2\pi f$$

$$E = mc^2$$

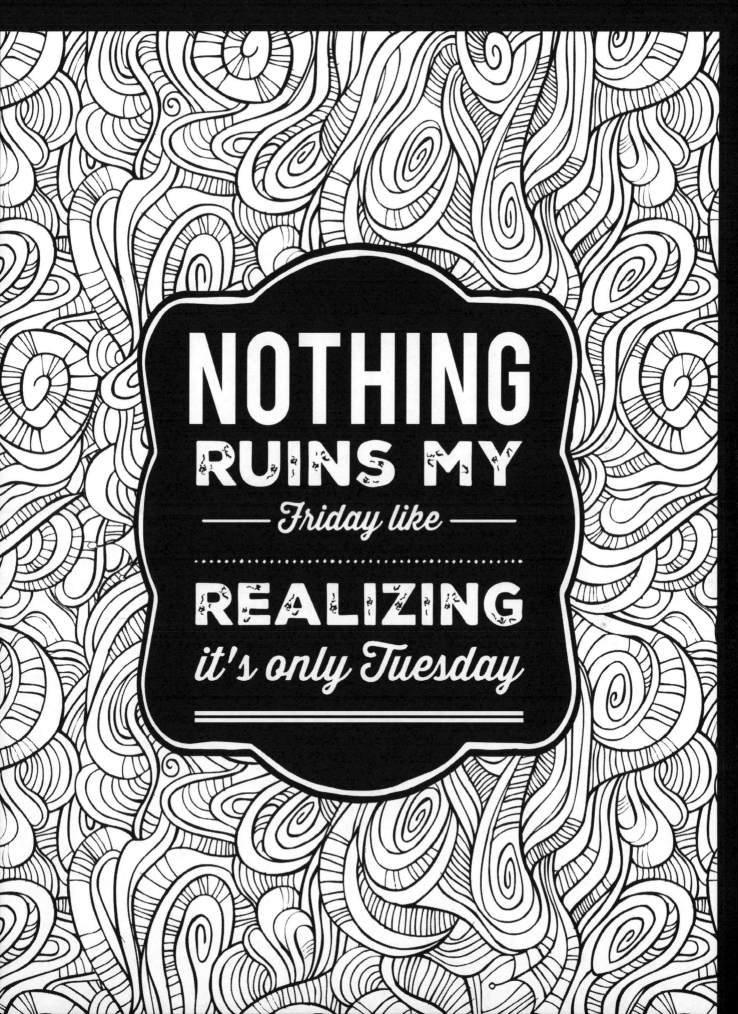

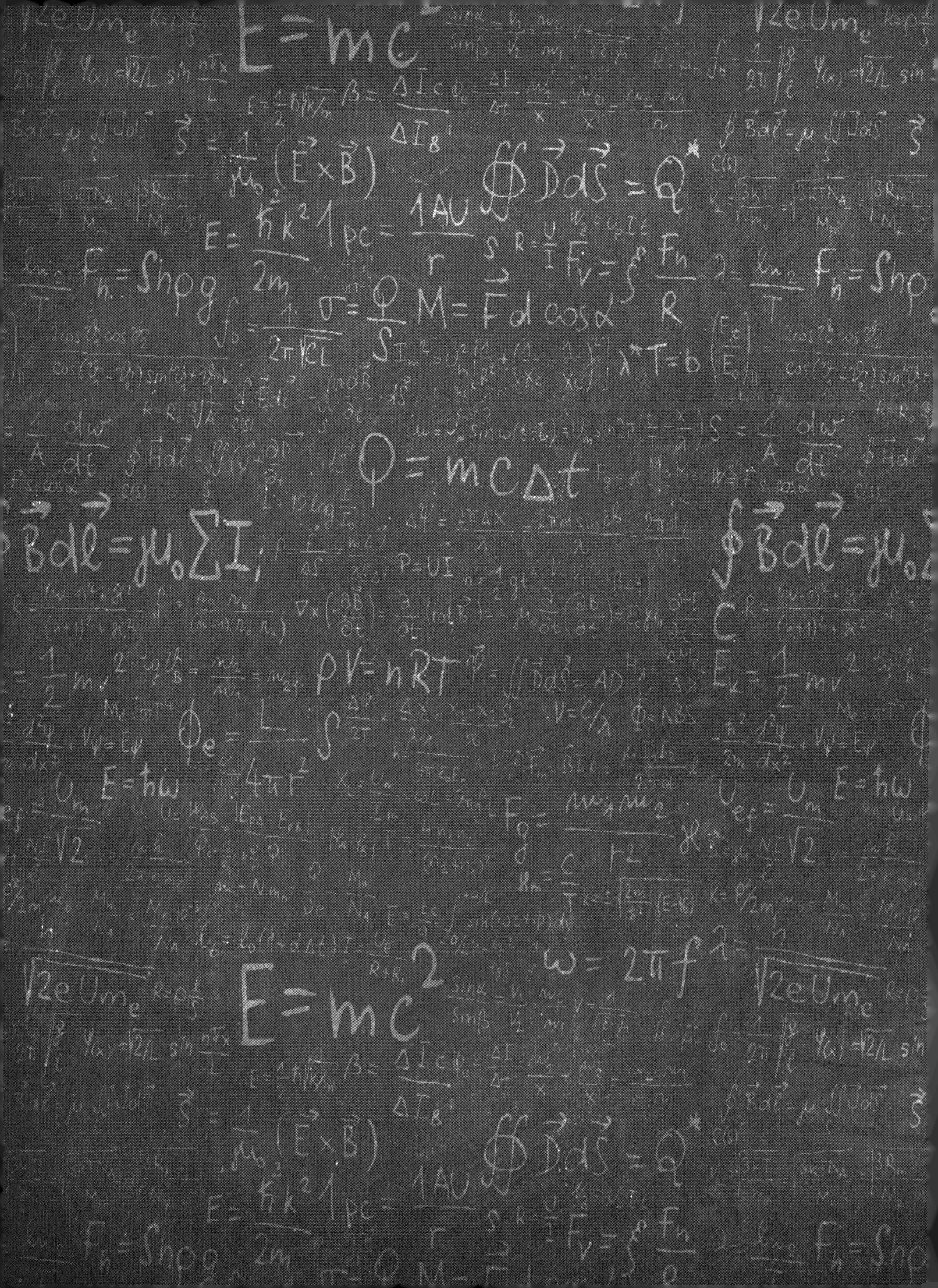
E=mc²
Q=mcΔt
ρV=nRT
ω=2πf
E=ħω
σ=Q/S
M=Fd cosα
λ*T=b
P=UI

$$E = mc^2$$

$$\oiint \vec{D}\,d\vec{S} = Q$$

$$\beta = \frac{\Delta I c}{\Delta I_B}$$

$$\vec{S} = \frac{1}{\mu_0}(\vec{E} \times \vec{B})$$

$$E = \frac{\hbar^2 k^2}{2m}$$

$$1pc = \frac{1AU}{r}$$

$$F_h = Sh\rho g$$

$$M = Fd\cos\alpha$$

$$\lambda^* T = b$$

$$Q = mc\Delta t$$

$$\oint \vec{B}\,d\vec{l} = \mu_0 \sum I_i$$

$$PV = nRT$$

$$E_k = \frac{1}{2}mv^2$$

$$E = \hbar\omega$$

$$\omega = 2\pi f$$

$$\sqrt{2eU_m}$$

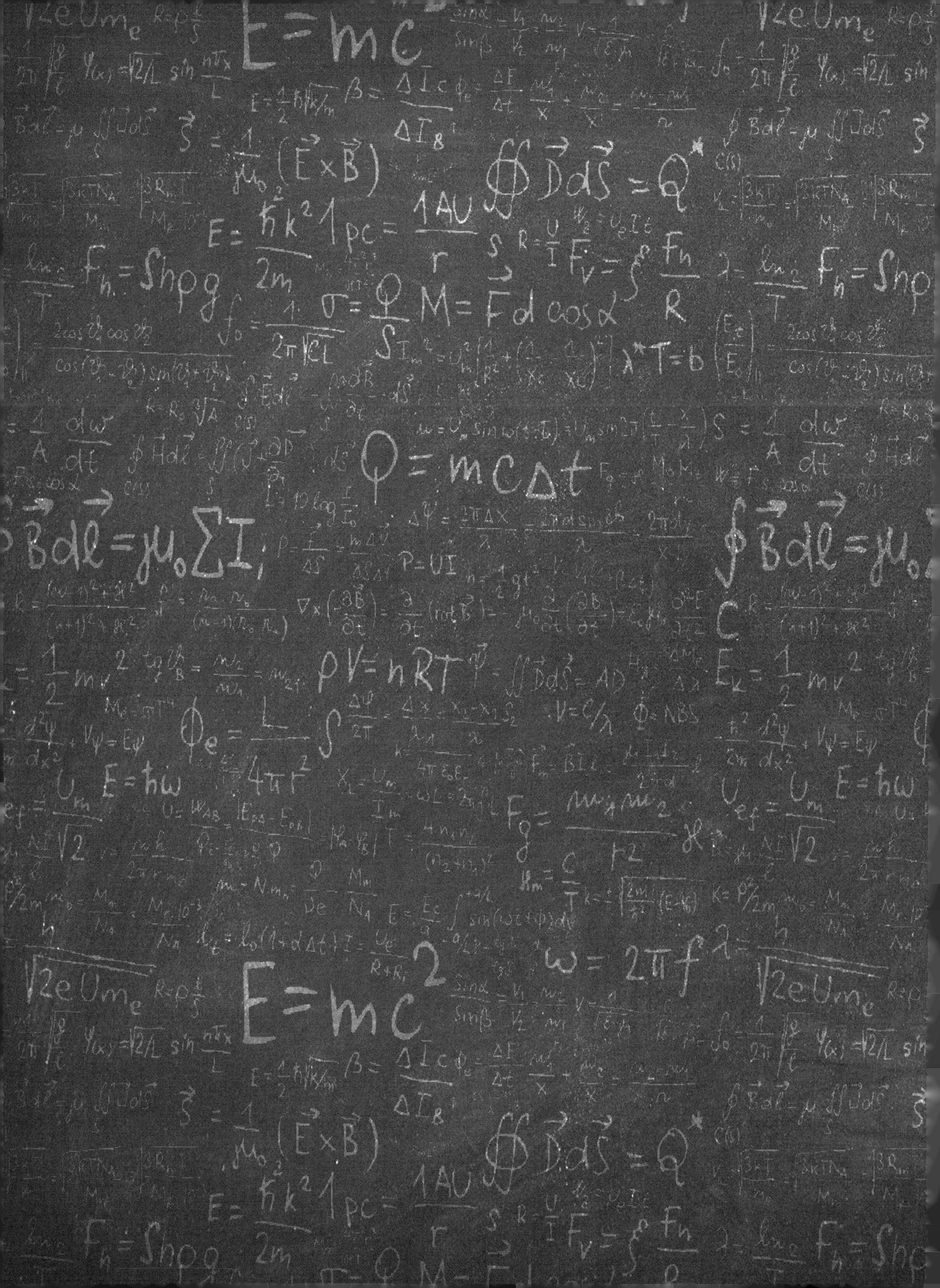
E=mc²
Q=mcΔt
pV=nRT
ω=2πf
E=ħω
1AU

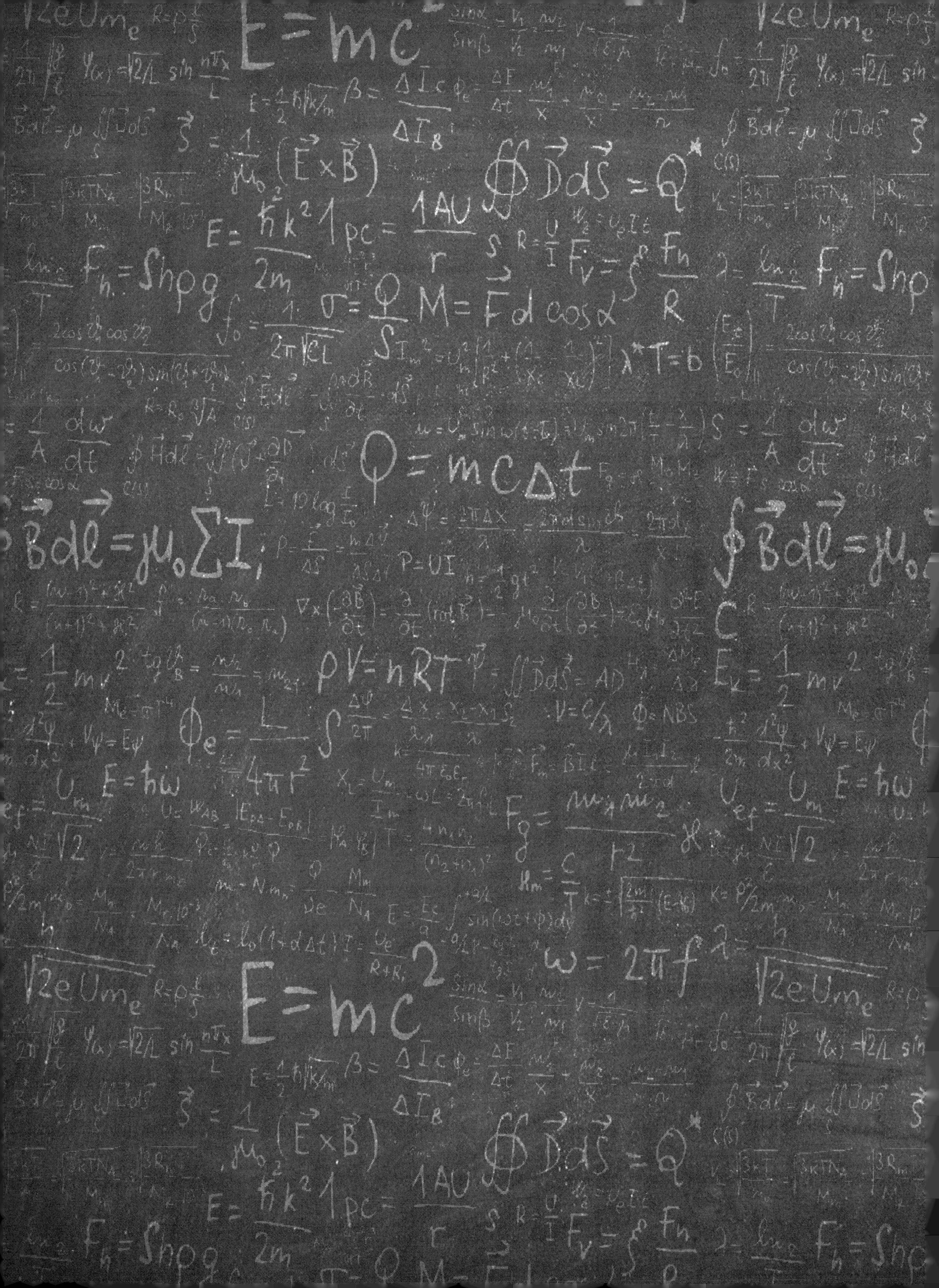
E=mc2
Q=mcΔt
pV=nRT
ω=2πf
E=ħω

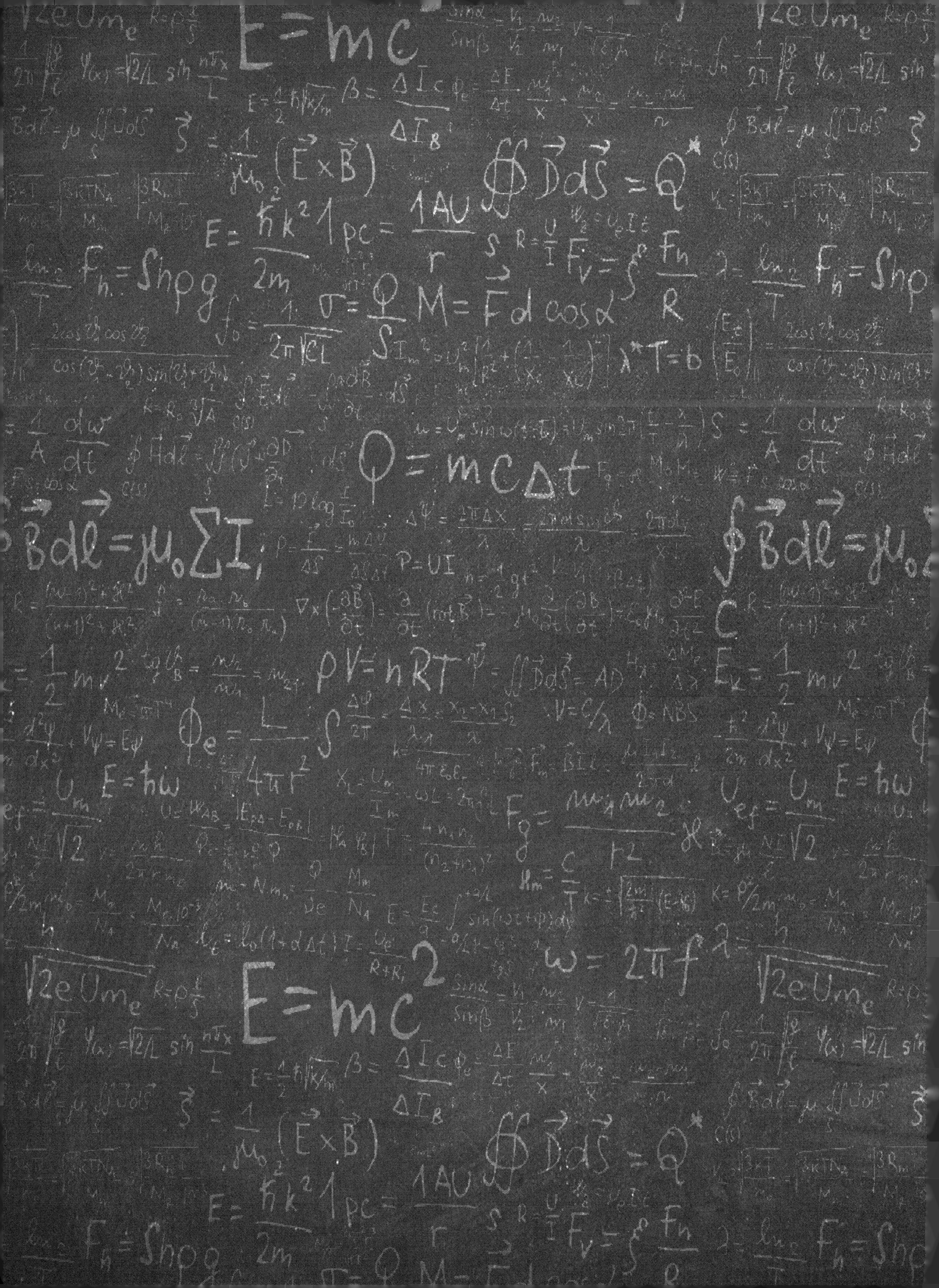
E=mc²
Q=mcΔt
pV=nRT
ω=2πf

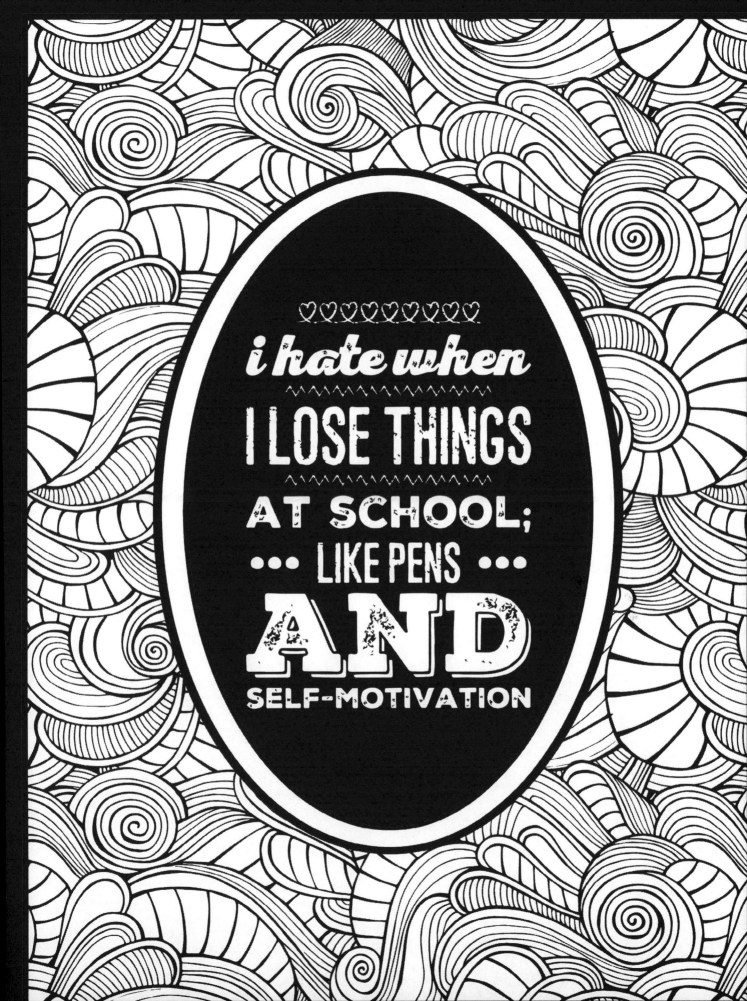

$$E = mc$$

$$\oint \vec{D}\, d\vec{S} = Q^*$$

$$E = \frac{\hbar k^2}{2m} \qquad pc = \frac{1\,AU}{r}$$

$$M = Fd\cos\alpha \qquad \lambda^* T = b$$

$$Q = mc\Delta t$$

$$\oint \vec{B}\, d\vec{\ell} = \mu_0 \sum I;$$

$$\oint \vec{B}\, d\vec{\ell} = \mu_0$$

$$PV = nRT$$

$$\frac{1}{2} m v^2 \qquad E_k = \frac{1}{2} m v$$

$$E = \hbar \omega \qquad E = \hbar \omega$$

$$E = mc^2 \qquad \omega = 2\pi f$$

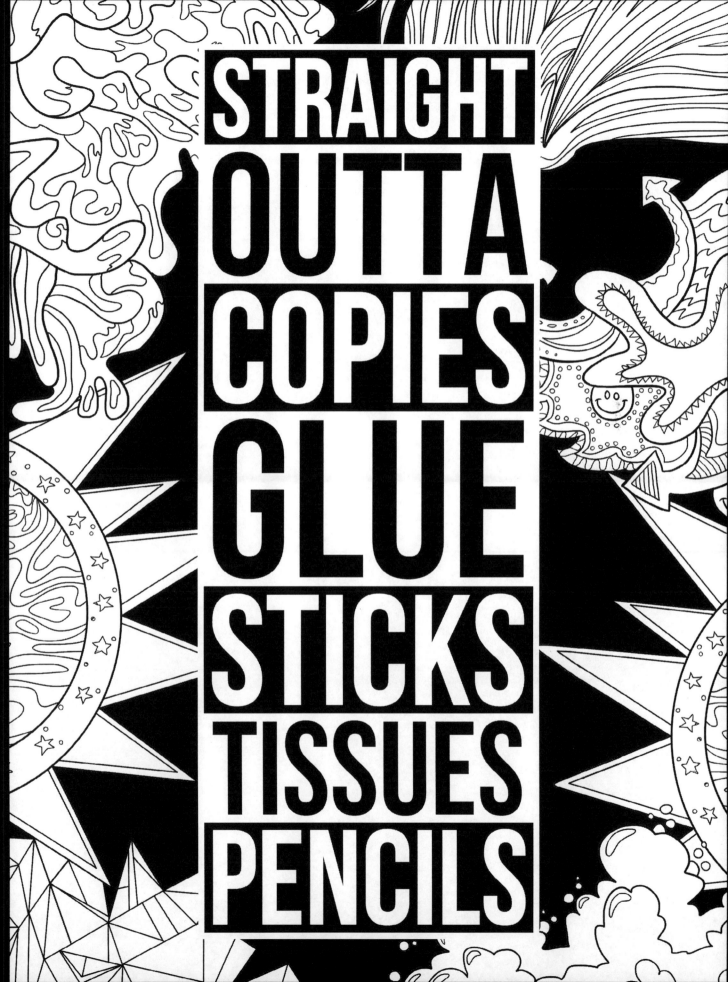

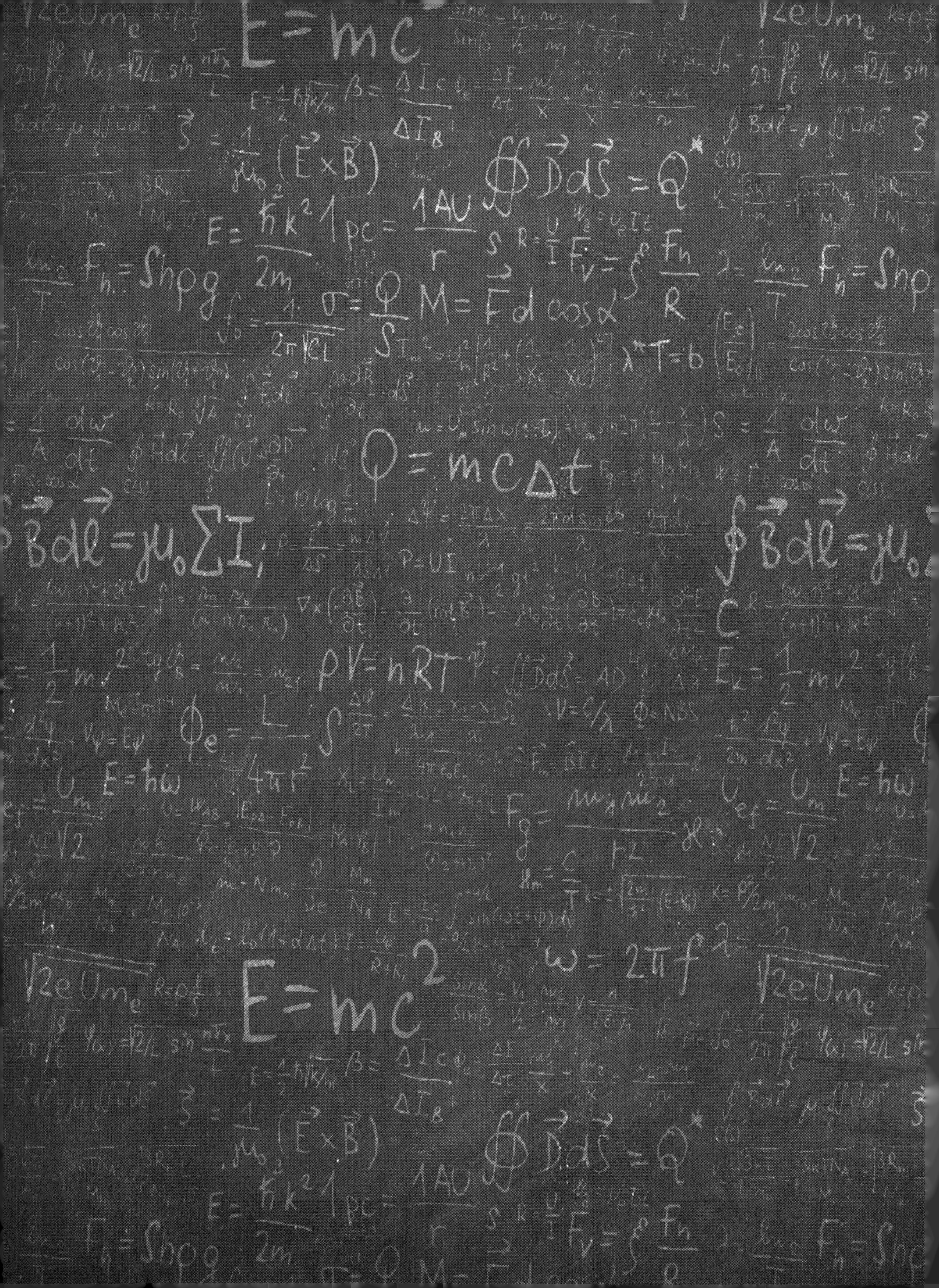
E=mc2
Q=mcΔt
pV=nRT
E=ħω
ω=2πf

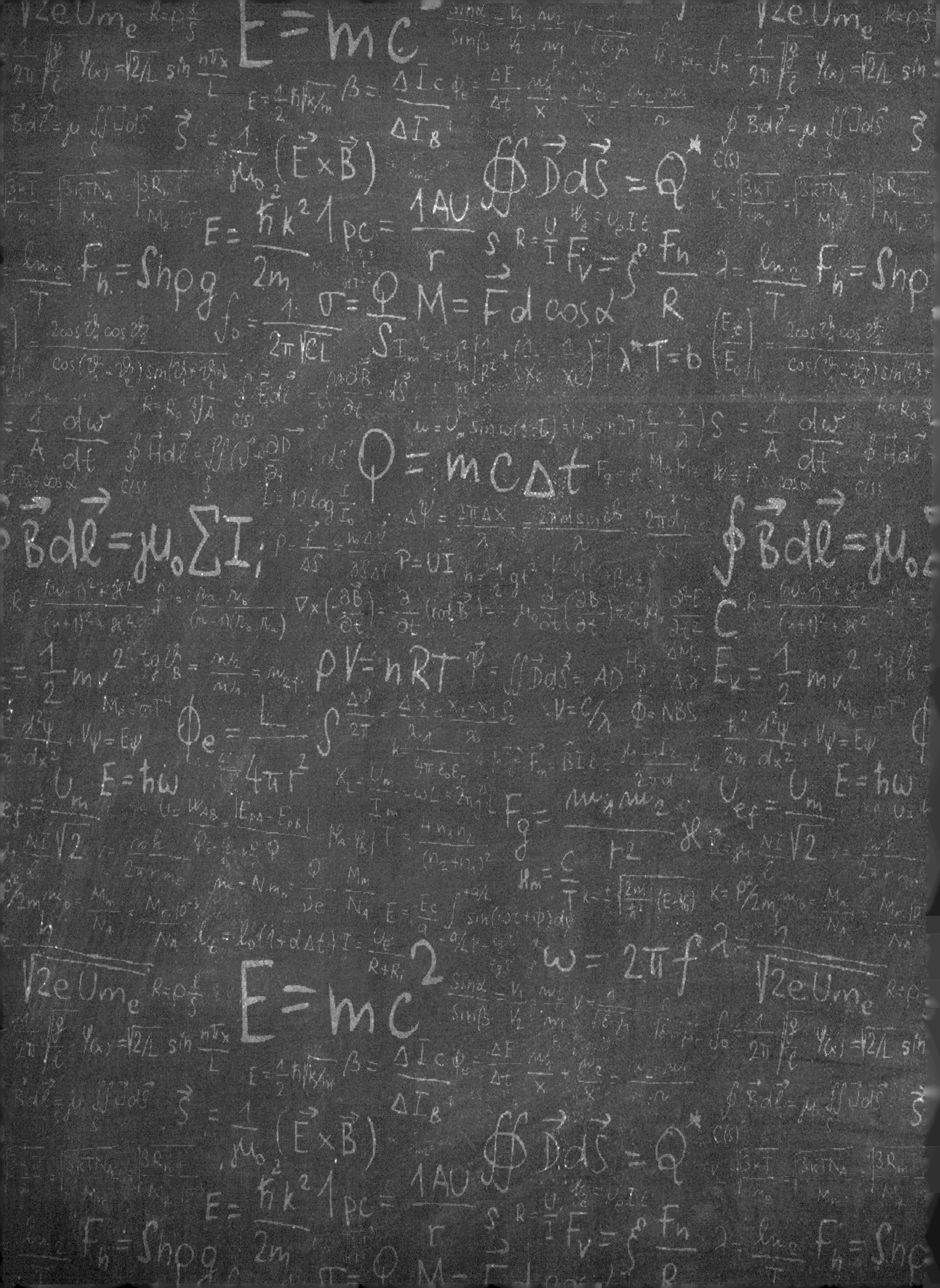
E=mc2
Q=mcΔt
pV=nRT
ω=2πf
E=ħω

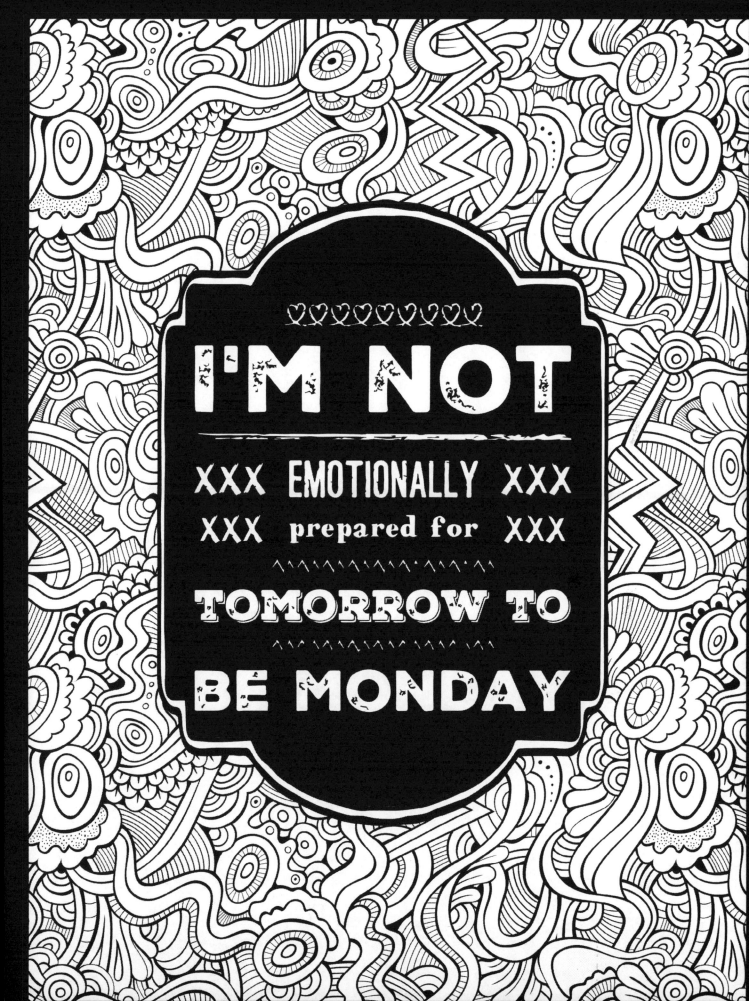

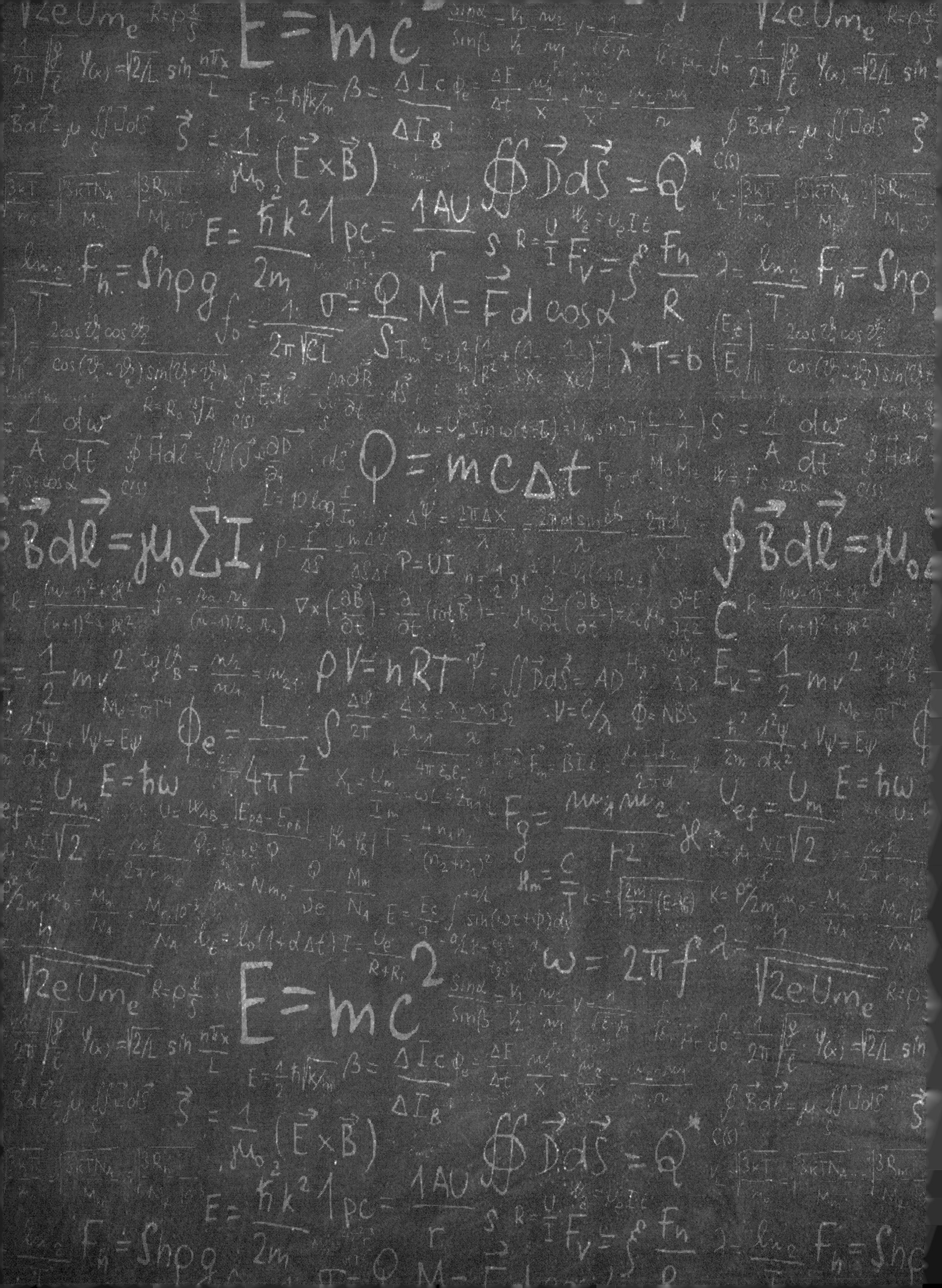
E=mc2
Q=mcΔt
pV=nRT
ω=2πf
P=UI
E=ħω

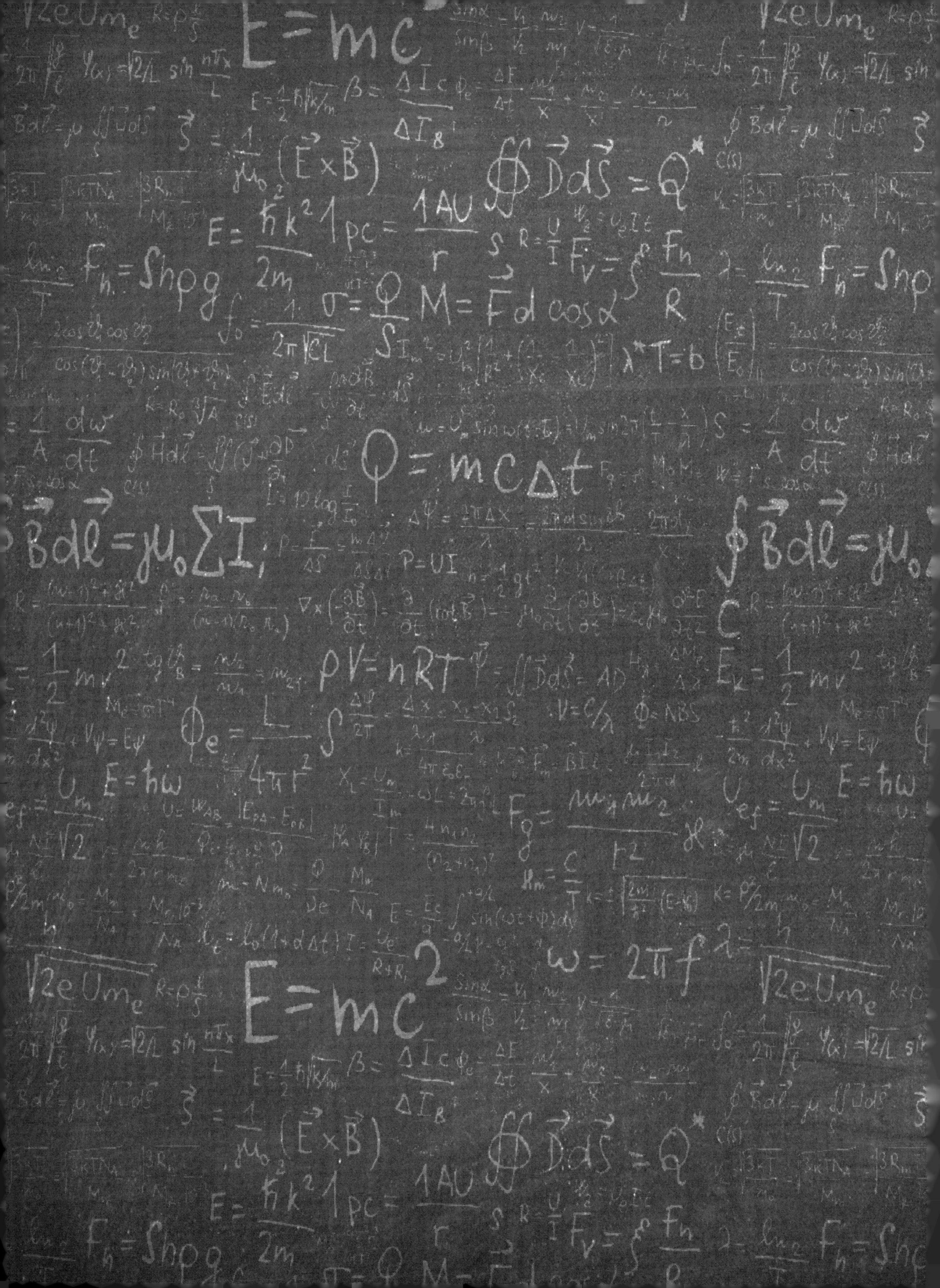
E=mc2
Q=mcΔt
pV=nRT
ω=2πf
E=ħω

# BE SURE TO FOLLOW US ON SOCIAL MEDIA FOR THE LATEST NEWS, SNEAK PEEKS, & GIVEAWAYS

[Instagram] @PapeterieBleu

[Facebook] Papeterie Bleu

[Twitter] @PapeterieBleu

# ADD YOURSELF TO OUR MONTHLY NEWSLETTER FOR FREE DIGITAL DOWNLOADS AND DISCOUNT CODES

www.papeteriebleu.com/newsletter

# CHECK OUT OUR OTHER BOOKS!

www.papeteriebleu.com

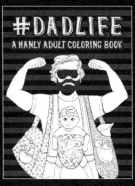
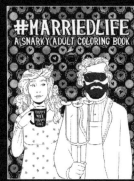

# CHECK OUT OUR OTHER BOOKS!

www.papeteriebleu.com

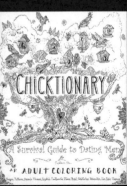

# CHECK OUT OUR OTHER BOOKS!

www.papeteriebleu.com

  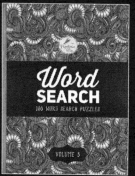 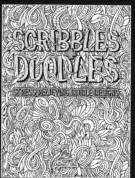 

Made in the USA
San Bernardino, CA
31 October 2017